WILBUR'S STORY
ADVENTURES OF A FEISTY FELINE

BY

LANY WILLIAMS

ILLUSTRATIONS BY PETR NESTRATOV

iUniverse, Inc.
New York Bloomington

Wilbur's Story
Adventures of a Feisty Feline

Copyright © 2008 by Lany Williams

All rights reserved. No part of this book may be used or reproduced by any means, graphic, electronic, or mechanical, including photocopying, recording, taping or by any information storage retrieval system without the written permission of the publisher except in the case of brief quotations embodied in critical articles and reviews.

The views expressed in this work are solely those of the author and do not necessarily reflect the views of the publisher, and the publisher hereby disclaims any responsibility for them.

iUniverse books may be ordered through booksellers or by contacting:

iUniverse
1663 Liberty Drive
Bloomington, IN 47403
www.iuniverse.com
1-800-Authors (1-800-288-4677)

Because of the dynamic nature of the Internet, any Web addresses or links contained in this book may have changed since publication and may no longer be valid. The views expressed in this work are solely those of the author and do not necessarily reflect the views of the publisher, and the publisher hereby disclaims any responsibility for them.

ISBN: 978-0-595-49847-5 (pbk)
ISBN: 978-0-595-61273-4 (ebk)

Printed in the United States of America

To all the animals in shelters who need loving homes.

Contents

Acknowledgments ix
Prologue..xi
Wilbur Comes Home to Live............................. 1
Ear Mites 5
Wild Animals.. 7
Kitty Door 11
The Great Flood.. 15
Babies.. 17
Welcome to the Neighborhood 19
Wilbur's Been Hit!.. 23
Bird Emergency.. 31
Cancer!.. 33
The Blizzard.. 35
Angel Boy 37
Wilbur and the Dangling Mouse 39
Baby Squirrel's First Outing 43
Wilbur and the Coyote...................................... 45
Wilbur's Lost! 49
About the Author: 53

Acknowledgments

Thanks to all my wonderful family, friends, and neighbors who advised and supported me in raising Wilbur. I could not have done it alone.

Prologue

As winter turns into spring, thoughts of expanding their family take hold of Lany and Jimmy. Adopting a kitten who's been abandoned or given away, needing someone to love and care for it, fills their minds. For them, it's exciting to think about bringing home their own baby cat to care for.

Lany had grown up in a household that included cats, a dog, chickens, mice, and turtles—you name it; they had it. Her mother had been a kindergarten teacher. At the end of each school year, she had brought home for the summer holiday whatever animal was currently residing in the classroom. Blossom and Chick-A-Boom had strutted their feathers in the backyard during those long, hot days. Lany's first cat, Mittens, was black with white paws, but unfortunately had to be given up for adoption because her brother and father were horribly allergic to cats. Jimmy'd had many cats in the past and missed having little furballs running around.

Lany and Jimmy scour the local animal shelters looking for a kitten to adopt. At this time of year, there aren't as many kittens available for adoption as there will be in the summer. Many shelters tell them to come back in a few months. Lany doesn't listen; she knows that special cat is out there just waiting for her to bring him home. That cat would be me, Wilbur!

But horror of all horrors, they almost end up with the wrong cat! Lany remembers seeing the most adorable six-week-old black kitty at the shelter in Salem. It is a quiet, dreary Saturday afternoon. There aren't many animals in the cages because most of them have already been adopted. A little black kitten, all by himself, is curled up in a ball in the back of the shelter. He looks up at Lany with big brown eyes. The kitten is exhausted from being picked up and handled all day. He is too young to have been abandoned by his mother. The staff tells Lany that he has been bottle-fed right up until that weekend. Her heart aches with tenderness for this little fluffball. With no kitten friends nearby and the dogs in the front of the shelter barking every now and then, the little guy cannot get his much-needed rest. He needs special loving care, which she is more than willing to give. Lany wants to scoop him up and take him home with her right then and there, but the shelter tells her that she needs to come back with all of the necessary paperwork before he can be hers. On the drive home, she even thinks of a name for the little guy, Spike.

It's too late to go back that day, so they drive back to the shelter the next afternoon. Oh no! Someone else came in before Lany and adopted Spike. (Phew, what a relief for me!) But she is so sad; she had his bed and toys all ready and waiting for him. Lany cries the whole drive home.

The next weekend, Lany is more determined than ever to find the kitty who is meant to be loved by her. Jimmy and Lany drive up to the MSPCA's shelter in Methuen. That's when they see me—and fall in love with me on sight.

Wilbur Comes Home to Live

Leaves on the trees are pale green with fresh new growth. The barn that houses the animal shelter sits on a little rise surrounded by fields of swaying grass and pastures of meandering horses. Lany feels excited because deep down she knows that she is about to find the little kitten that is meant for her.

They park in the lot and walk into the office; the volunteers who are working that weekend direct them through the barn to the cat area in the back. Bright sunshine flows through the windows into every nook and cranny. There are a few dogs barking in the distance, but the noise isn't overwhelming or too scary for any of us in the back room.

Upon entering the room, Lany turns to her right and sees me, a little orange tiger-striped kitten, peeking out through the bars of my cage and looking inquisitively all around. This is big stuff here; the world as I've known it is about to change. I'm not afraid of the people approaching me. All of the activity is great entertainment. My brother is asleep on the blanket behind me.

When my brother and I were five weeks old, someone found our home under their front porch steps and brought us to this big cozy barn. My furry mother was nowhere to be seen. All I wanted was a warm place to lay my head and good food to eat. Having my brother with me made it a lot less scary.

Now I am ten weeks old and ready to be out on my own. Lany picks me up, and I am content to sit in her arms looking around. Little does she know, I am not normally this mild mannered. It must be getting close to nap time.

The overhead ceiling fan fascinates me as I watch it go round and round with a soft whirring noise. The nice people in the barn tell Lany my name is Wilbur, after the pig in *Charlotte's Web*. A pig! Who wants to be named after a pig? I hope she changes it to Rocky or Hulk, something big and tough, but no such luck.

"Wilbur. I love that name. It fits him perfectly," she says. Grrr.

With a narrow chin, flat head, and two little pointy ears, I look—and feel—very devilish. I tear around the cage, pouncing upon my unsuspecting brother and chasing him until we are both pooped. Lany wants to take me and my little brother home with her, so we can keep each other company when we're alone in the house, but no such luck. A family with a little boy is one step ahead of her; they take my little black and white brother. It's for the best. We probably would have messed up the house pretty bad if left to our own devices.

Before setting out that day, Lany made sure she had all of the necessary paperwork with her so they could take me home right away. She isn't going through that heartache again. I now have a new mom and dad. I sit in luxury on a soft blankie in the middle of the backseat, as I watch the road fly by through the windows. This is so cool, although the trees moving by real fast out the side window make my stomach feel a little queasy. But I'm a trooper; I don't get sick.

Once at my new home, I'm given the run of the house—and boy, do I run. Mom and Dad follow behind me. I don't go near Dad because of his huge feet: I think he'll squash me. Mom tells Dad to take off his big sneakers so his feet won't appear so intimidating. I'm barred from the basement. They believe I could easily get lost down there with all of the dark corners and boxes of stuff.

Cornered in Mom's office on the second floor, I am blocked from escaping when they close the door. Being very inquisitive, I nose around the room a bit. After checking everything out, I sit in Mom's lap and fall asleep, purring like a giant Mack truck.

Oh boy, toys! Over the last few days, Mom has bought me stuffed mice that I pounce upon as I pretend that I'm the big bad hunter. Yeah, that be me. When it's time to eat, I pick up a mousey and carry it with me, spitting it out beside the bowl, though sometimes it lands in the food. No big deal. I just chew it all up together. By the end of the day, there's a little line of mousies beside my bowl. Miss Pinkie is my favorite. She's all chewed to pieces, but I love her anyway.

At night I climb up on the bed with Mom. As she strokes my fur, I bite her hands. Isn't that what bedtime is for? She's so upset that she asks Dad why her new kitty always bites her in bed.

He laughs and says, "Wilbur and I play on the bed in the morning after you go to work. We roughhouse: I roll and push him around while he fights back by kicking and biting me."

To make me stop biting, Mom fills a spray bottle with water and sprays it at me. That is not nice! Why is my mom doing this to me? I am not happy. I fly off the bed and dive underneath. She coaxes me back out by calling, "Wilbur." But when I see the spray bottle on the bedside table, I take off running. I skid down the stairs in my haste, toenails scrabbling on the hardwood floor as I fly around the corner. But Mom doesn't want me afraid of her, so she comes up with another idea.

One night, Mom has had enough of the biting, so after going to bed, she puts me out of the bedroom and shuts the door. She wakes up soon after to Dad coming up the stairs, laughing his head off.

"Meow, meow!" I cry piteously. I became wedged under the bedroom door while trying to get back into the bedroom. Can't she hear me meowing for crying out loud?! But I guess those bright orange rubber things she puts in her ears at night keep her from hearing me.

When Dad opens the door, I must have looked like a little dust mop sweeping the hardwood floor because I am sprawled flat between the door and the floor. Dad finally rescues me and scoops me up in his arms. God forbid he laughs at me. I'm very sensitive you know.

The usual nightly ritual is for me to get on the bed, go up to Mom's head, and stick my head under her hair by her neck. I'm sad and miss my real mom. In a trance, I purr like a little engine and begin to drool while thinking that I'm back on my furry mom's belly. Mom thinks I'm sucking on her hair. She doesn't want me eating her hair, so she pushes me away.

"Hey, why can't I snuggle up with you?" I whimper. I go right back for more.

After many nights of this, Mom asks other people if their cats eat hair. She finds out that I'm kneading her head, like I would my mother's belly, to try and get milk. This happens when kittens are taken away from their mothers too soon. Like I said, I miss my furry mom. Mom makes sure she keeps my toenails clipped because my kitten claws are pretty sharp on her head. Toenail clipping is a trip in itself, which will be explained later. To this day, I still knead Mom's head. It's therapy for me.

After the kneading is done, I stop by the nightstand for a sip of water. I stick my head in the water glass to take a drink. Sometimes it's pretty hard to reach the water, so I stick my whole head in the glass to reach the bottom. I'm sure I look pretty funny with my head in the glass. My eyes feel like they're bugging out while I stretch my tongue out to reach the water. I don't like my own water bowl downstairs. It's not as fun as drinking from a glass. Mom tells me to buzz off, but when this doesn't work she finally brings me my own glass to drink out of. My glass is short, so I don't have to stick my whole head in to reach the water, very thoughtful of her. After getting a drink, I jump down and get in my own bed by the hot air vent. It's like having my own personal sauna. Mmmm.

My bed is Mom's old laundry basket that I appropriated. Laundry time becomes playtime. Mom annoyingly dangles socks in front of my face, so I bat at them to get them away. Then she throws clothes over me, and I have to claw my way out from under the pile. Mom's lucky one of those claws doesn't sink into her hand. After playtime, I fall asleep in the basket. Mom ended up getting another laundry basket. It was just easier all around.

If Mom gets up during the night to use the bathroom, I drag my body out of bed to follow her into the bathroom. She picks me up and places me on her lap. I sit and sway and almost fall over as I'm barely awake, but I always get up with her. I don't want to let her out of my sight: I don't want to lose her like I did my furry mom and brother.

Ear Mites

At my first checkup, the vet tells Mom that I have ear mites, tiny little bugs that live in the ear canal. Ugh! Mom noticed I was constantly digging at my ears and leaving dried blood flaked all over my bed. When scratching at my ears, I get this really funny look on my face as my eyes roll up into my head from the relief. It feels like heaven.

Mom's amazed at how good I am for Dr. Thistle. "Why can't you be as well behaved at home?" she asks.

"Well, if you had taken away the itch, then I would have behaved better," I think to myself. I stare out the window watching the birds fly around the bushes as the doctor pokes my belly and inspects my eyes, ears, and mouth. I just want to get outside to chase all those birds around. In the end, Dr. Thistle gives Mom some drops to put in my ears to kill the bugs.

The medicine stings when Mom first tries to put it in, and I want no part of that. I wriggle free from her arms and take off like a shot to hide under the bed. I hear Mom hunting for me, checking all my usual haunts within the house. But she finds me. Dang, that woman's good. Mom holds my body tight to her chest to get me back to the kitchen where my medicine is waiting.

"Okay, how do I get Wilbur to hold still while I swab a cotton ball in both of his ears?" Mom muses out loud.

She sits on me. Oh, the indignity!

Mom gets the cotton ball ready with the liquid and kneels on the floor, putting me between her knees. You have to understand; I am only a little bigger than a softball at this time. I squirm backward, but she closes her heels together to close me in. I'm so mad at her. It's very undignified to be sat upon. When she's done torturing me, I stalk off with my tail straight up in the air.

"Wilbur, come back," she laughs at me.

"Keep talking to the tail," I growl and continue to stalk away.

Besides the ear swabbing, Mom also sits on me to clip my toenails or to give me medicine with an eyedropper. I hate those times.

Mom finally finds an alternative to sitting on me when forcing me to take my medicine. It all started when Dad made himself a sandwich with deli meat. While making his sandwich, I jump up on the counter to check out what he's doing and stick my nose right in the sandwich. Dad pushes me off, but ends up giving me little pieces of turkey to eat, thus starting my lifelong love affair with deli meat.

To this day, if Mom wants me in the house and I drag my feet, she grabs the plastic deli bag and shakes it out the back door. I come running when I hear the rustling plastic. Yummm. Mom always keeps deli meat on hand, just in case. It's really good with medicine on it, as the medicine tastes just like bubblegum. I scarf it all up without a second thought; it's much better than being sat upon.

Wild Animals

They keep me inside for the first nine months of my life. Mom and Dad say it's so I won't get eaten by wild animals. Right. Suburban Boston, wild animals. Ha!

I don't mind being inside because Mom works from home a lot, and I hang out with her in her office. That little darting arrow on the computer screen is fun to chase, though stepping on those moving keys sure messes up the project she's working on. After getting bored with that, I climb up on the guest room bed to snooze in the cozy comforter.

Mom buys lots of toys for me. Besides my mousies, I also have stuffed animals that Mom bought me on her travels. She always brings me home a little something. The first time she does this, she comes home with a little stuffed cat that looks just like me. I beat it up because Mom is more interested in it than in me. I am jealous. Mom even calls it *Baby Wilbur*. Enough of that. I beat up on that thing every chance I get by biting its head and kicking at it with my back feet. I'm pretty strong and tough you know. Mom has to put Baby Wilbur up out of my sight so that I'll calm down and not go after it. Nowadays, I cuddle up with all of my toys when I nap. But Baby Wilbur is still up out of reach. Good riddance.

Mom and I have playtime every day: I chase her around the dining room table, or she chases me. It's times like these that I miss my brother.

Sometimes I'll be looking behind me to see where she is, and I'll run right into a wall.

"Oh my God," Mom gasps, bent over double laughing.

I am not amused. As I mentioned earlier, I do not like to be laughed at.

Sometimes Mom hides on the stairway; she jumps out and yells, "Boo!" when I come racing around the corner. Man does she scare the heck out of me. I fly up in the air with my fur fluffed out and take off running. Secretly I love being scared. If Mom's relaxing in the living room, I jump up on the arm of the couch, stick my nose in her ear, and run off, begging her to chase me.

When Mom and Dad believe I am finally old enough to be let outside, it's a beautiful crisp November day. The leaves lie all golden brown on the grass, just waiting to be picked up. What fun to jump into the piles of raked leaves. Mom throws more leaves on top of me while I burrow down underneath, kind of like laundry time.

When wandering about, I don't go any farther than I can see them, so they feel pretty good about letting me out. There's a small round thing on the front porch steps; I go over to investigate. Mom says, "That is so cute," and has to have a picture of me sitting next to this thing called a pumpkin. I am the same size and color as the pumpkin, but with pale green eyes. Ever since that day she calls me her *Pumpkin Boy*.

Our house has three outside doors: the front, the kitchen, and the basement. Mom tries to get me used to going in and out through the basement. She doesn't want me to take off when she or Dad comes home through the front door. Now that I have a taste of freedom, I want out. I jump on Mom and bite her to get her attention, then I run for the basement door, clearly indicating that she should follow me to let me out. Well, she tires long before I do with going up and down the basement stairs, so she starts letting me out through the other doors.

When I am outside, I make friends in the neighborhood with the other kitties. Mom calls me *Mr. Hit and Run*. As she watches one day out the living room window, another cat is in our yard sitting on top of the picnic table. I'm underneath the table and reach up to swat at the other kitty, then I take off. I want him to chase me like my brother used to. The other cat ignores me. I'm sure he's thinking, "Just ignore it and it will go away."

I also enjoy watching the neighborhood kids play. The moms go out late in the morning to chat and drink coffee while the preschoolers run around screaming and yelling. One child spots me and runs after me, but I dart just out of reach. One day while Mom is in her office, she hears the kids crying, "Fox, fox!" As she looks out the window, a fox tears through my backyard with a bunch of four-year-olds hot on his tail. Mom makes me stay in for days after that.

Kitty Door

Mom thinks it's smart of her to start letting me out in November; the weather will be getting colder, and snow will soon start to fly. She believes I'll want to stay inside when that happens. Wrong! That first snow fall, I'm outside doing face plows in the snow. I stick my whole head in and come up shaking so that snow flies in all directions. Man I love the snow. I want out all the time, no matter what the weather. I even want out in rainstorms.

Mom gets tired of my jumping on her in the middle of the night to let me out. She rigs a window in the living room with a little flap of plastic that I can push through to get in and out on my own. Mom doesn't own the house, so she can't cut a kitty door in the back door. The flap works pretty well for quite awhile, until springtime that is.

Mom's friend, Eva, comes to visit her one day. While they're sitting in the living room, I pop in through the kitty door. Boy do they startle me, and I'm sure I startle them, but, what the heck, I come in anyway.

Eva says to Mom, "I didn't know Wilbur had one leg bigger than the other!"

Mom says, "He doesn't."

Sure enough, my right front leg is swollen. Mom picks me up and feels the leg. It doesn't hurt me, but I want down. It's very undignified to be scooped up in front of strangers.

Mom makes a frantic phone call to her sister—the expert on all things cat since I now have five kitty cousins—who says to leave the leg alone for a few days. If it doesn't go back to normal, then Mom is to call Dr. Thistle. Eventually, the leg does go back to normal size. Mom never figures out what caused the leg to swell up. My guess is that those nasty little buzzing things under the front porch steps had something to do with it. One of them hurt me when I stepped on it. I never paid much attention to them before, but I now give those bees a wide berth when using the front door.

By this time, Dad has moved out of our house and into his own. I miss him a lot; besides giving me turkey to eat, he tussled and played with me. Mom likes to cuddle all the time. Yuck.

One morning Mom wakes up and rolls over in bed to find a mouse, actually a flattened mouse, right next to her pillow. Ewww! She must have rolled over during the night and squished it in her sleep. She flies out of bed yelling, "Wilbur!"

"Oh good, Mom found the present I left for her." I'm downstairs having breakfast before heading back outside to find some more goodies to bring her.

Mom's *perpetrator* is long gone. She sighs, grabs a handful of tissues, and picks up the dead mouse by its tail. While it swings in the air, she takes it downstairs and shudders as she throws it in the trash. She immediately takes all the sheets off the bed and, along with her PJ's, puts everything in the wash. I don't think she appreciated my gift. Other days, Mom finds dead mice on the front hall stairs, treasures that didn't quite make it up to the bedroom before expiring.

The final straw that closed my kitty door for good happened after Janie moved in with us. Our neighbor Louise works with Janie and knew she was looking for a place to live. She also knew that Mom was looking for a roommate, so she introduced them to each other. After Mom gets home from work one night, she hears an interesting story from Janie.

"I was minding my own business when I realized a bird was flying about in the house. Wilbur had caught it and probably thought he had killed it, but it got away from him. I began screaming and screaming. Louise was in her backyard, so I hung my head out the window and called for her. I sounded like I was being attacked! Louise ran over with dog biscuits, thinking that if Wilbur had the bird in his mouth, he might drop it and eat the biscuits. What! Dog biscuits for a cat? Okay ... whatever. Well, Louise came well equipped: she had dog biscuits *and* a box. We finally caught the bird. It was pretty easy, but still exciting."

Wilbur's Story

Louise had her own version of that same event: "I was just sitting down on the patio with a glass of iced tea when I heard this little voice from above. It wasn't like God calling me, more like a little angel. I couldn't figure out what the angel was saying, so I got up and walked to the front yard. Then I heard Janie calling from the upstairs window; the *angel* was in a panic. I went in the front door. Wilbur and a bird were under the bed. Smart me, I went home to get dog biscuits and a shoebox. The bird was now hiding behind Lany's suitcase. Janie saved the day, though I am sure the dog biscuits were invaluable."

Mom comes home a little after all this happened to a calm house. Later on that night, she has her own bird encounter. I bring her another bird that I caught outside. One for Janie and one for Mom—I didn't want to disappoint Mom. The bird is stunned into immobility. After shutting me in her office, Mom grabs a shoebox from her closet, dumps out the shoes, scoops up the bird using the top of the box, and runs outside. She places the bird on a large flat rock in the backyard. Another bird released back into the wild. Mom hopes it isn't too traumatized to fly away. Needless to say, the kitty door is permanently shut after that fiasco.

The Great Flood

One day in March, Mom left to go to Connecticut for business. I am inside because there was a massive snowstorm, and then it rained on top of it. She gets home around 6:00 PM that night. I greet her at the door, but rather than trying to get outside, I run to the top of the cellar stairs. Mom thinks this is strange because I usually go out the front door. So she says, "What the heck, might as well follow and check it out."

By six o'clock on an early March day it's pretty dark and cold outside. She turns on the cellar light to check downstairs and muses, "That's strange. Why is Wilbur's litter box floating by the cellar stairs?"

The whole basement is flooded from the rain and snow! I had to hold my bladder all day because I couldn't get to my litter box. Poor me!

Fascinated by the whole thing, I follow Mom down the stairs to check it out. Although I'm not stupid enough to go in the water, Mom is. She rolls up her pants, takes off her shoes, and plunges in. Eight inches of melted snow in March is freezing! She wades over to the far corner of the gloomy and very wet basement where the pump to drain the water is located. The pump is caught on the edge of the hole. Mom reaches down to free the pump, and it starts right up again. Fuming, she has visions of electrocuting herself in the water, but what else is she supposed to do? The one good thing is that the house is a rental. The property manager comes

Lany Williams

over with wet vacs and fans to dry out the basement without leaving a stinky mildew mess behind.

That weekend Mom throws away a ton of cherished mementos. I have a ball running in and out of all the boxes stacked up in the backyard. I pop up out of one and dive into another. Mom makes sure I don't get thrown out with all the trash.

Babies

On a warm summer day, Mom opened all the windows to catch a breeze while cleaning the house. I'm outside playing, and she's in the living room running the vacuum. A few minutes later, she happens to glance out the window. There I am sitting in the grass in the backyard, and I'm looking at the ground by my feet. "What is he looking at?" she ponders.

Mom goes out the front door and moves quietly around to the side of the house. I don't hear her. When she gets close, she says sharply, "Wilbur!"

I look up as if asking, "What?" So does the baby mouse at my feet.

Two pairs of innocent eyes look up at Mom: one is curious; the other is scared to death and pleading. She scoops me up and hauls me back inside, wriggling all the way. No fair! I was having a blast. That little furry thing keeps moving, and I keep dragging it back. It's much more fun than those mousies in my toy box that don't go anywhere.

Mom finishes cleaning the house, then she goes back out to see if the baby mouse has scampered away. No. He looks like he's waiting for his mother to come get him and is too afraid to move. The baby mouse is curled up into a little brown furry ball. Mom sighs, "I can't leave him here. Another cat will come along and eat him."

She opens the garage and finds an old teacup to scoop the mouse up in and puts on an old pair of gloves. The baby mouse doesn't even try to run away when she approaches with the cup.

"You poor thing, you're quivering. Your mother must be worried sick about you," she says. Mom knows she'd be horrified if I was threatened by a ferocious wild animal. My face, plastered up against the window, stares with fascination at her running around outside with the mouse.

Mom's idea is to leave the mouse in the cup on the garage floor. He never moves when she gently places the cup on the dirt floor. She leaves the garage door cracked an inch, so that his mom can get in, or he can get out. She hopes there isn't enough room for me or any other mouse-eating predator to get in. All night she lies in bed worrying about that poor defenseless mouse shut in that dirty old garage.

When Mom goes out to the garage the next day, the baby mouse is gone. She sure hopes it was his mother who found him. No big deal to me. I know where there are loads of other baby mice to be found: I know where the nest is.

Welcome to the Neighborhood

    The people who own the house where Mom, Janie, and I live have decided to move back in. Now is a good time for Mom to find a house of our own, with Janie, of course, coming with us. Mom spends months looking for just the right place: one that has lots of room for me to run around, both inside and out.

    She finally finds a house in Woburn. A friend tells her to take me over to the new house, so that I can check it out and be a little familiar with it before we are there for good. She puts me in my carrier, takes me into the empty house, and lets me roam at will. Hmmm. This is interesting. I am not allowed in the attic or basement; she doesn't want to worry about getting me back out. I behave very well on our visit.

    When Mom comes looking for me, we meet face-to-face in the bathroom. I found one of the only places in the house that is high off the ground, the shelf above the bathroom sink. It is much safer to be up high, in case a surprise attack happens.

    When we first move into the new house, Mom keeps me inside, partly because it is the dead of winter and very cold outside and partly because it's a new neighborhood with unknown kitties lurking outside. After a few weeks, I'm ready to go out. I let her know by jumping on her leg when she walks by me. I dig in with my claws and take a good bite while

I'm at it. Because it is winter, I don't have much neighborhood competition to contend with, but come springtime, oh boy.

One of our neighbors is a huge dark gray cat. He looks very tough with part of an ear missing and matted fur. He stalks down the street, I swear, looking for trouble. It seems as if the earth trembles when he's out prowling around. I'm ready to defend my turf. This is my new home you bully. Stay away. Hisss!

When Mom hears the loud screeching and hissing, she comes running outside to break up the fight. I am pretty loud as I defend my territory; I can tell you. The bully and I face off at either end of Mom's car in the driveway. The *clash of the titans* ensues underneath the car. There's a loud thud when one of us smacks up against the tailpipe. Ooh, that hurts. Fur flies, both gray and orange.

Mom grabs the broom and races outside. She whacks at us two combatants, trying to get us back to our opposite ends of the car. Oh no, the spray bottle! Both of us bound into the backyard as we run away from the dreaded bottle. I still hate it when she gets out the spray bottle, even when she is just cleaning the house.

One weekend in March, I'm not feeling good, so I decide to lie on the couch. It's a nice day, but I have no interest in going outside. Mom stops to pet me, but I just growl at her. I am hurting from one of the many cat fights that I've had recently. Usually I would just swipe at Mom if I didn't want to be bothered. She lets me be, but notices that I'm pretty lethargic for a few days.

By the end of the week, I snuggle on Janie's bed amongst the pillows, which is unusual because I'm not allowed in her room. Mom sees me; I know I shouldn't be in there, so I jump off the bed. There is blood all over the comforter and pillows.

"Oh my God, Wilbur!" Mom is horrified.

She calls my doctor. The office is closed, but there is a phone number for emergencies. She calls it, and they tell her to bring me right in. She immediately scoops me up, puts me in my carrier, and takes me to the emergency room.

During the drive there, I am really good and do not make any noise. I blink at Mom to let her know that I love her and appreciate her racing to the hospital to make me better. She grips the steering wheel tightly for the entire forty-five minute drive. It seems to take forever.

The vet tells Mom that I was bitten in the butt by another cat. How embarrassing! I've been in pain for days, but Mom never realized it. Cat bites can leave a poison under the skin that is toxic until drained. Luckily, the abscess ruptured on its own. The vet shaves my butt and puts medicine on the wound to help it heal. Then she gives Mom a large plastic cone to put around my head, so that I won't lick off the medication and make myself ill.

When we get home, Mom carries me up to the bedroom, closes the door, and tries to put the cone on me while I struggle to keep that from happening. What is this big white thing wrapped around my neck and blocking my vision?

Immediately, I try to run and hide under the bed, which ends up turning the cone inside out and freaking me out. I take off like a shot, trying to get away from this thing that is attached to me. My eyes are big and round and looking at Mom for help. I see she's trying hard not to laugh while also trying to grab hold of me. Not funny.

Once she nabs me, the cone is history. When Mom pulls it off and opens the bedroom door, I fly out of there like a rocket and hide for hours. Mom never finds me. She feels bad for Janie and her nice bedding and offers to dry clean or replace it. Janie's a trooper; she says not to worry and cleans it herself. Whether she knows it or not, Janie is my unofficial godmother for all of the loving care she has always shown me.

A few years and many cat fights later, the bully cat leaves the neighborhood. Mom actually felt sorry for him whenever she saw him out on the street in the coldest of weather. She only hopes that he has as loving a home as I do. Purrr.

Wilbur's Been Hit!

Shortly after the butt-biting incident, I suffer another tragedy in my short life. It's a rainy Friday evening in June, rather gloomy, but kids are playing out in the street anyway. Janie has a friend over, and Mom's getting ready to head down to her friend Rob's house. Traffic goes very fast down my road: the mothers are constantly yelling at drivers to slow down. I hear the loud screeching of tires—and then SMACK!

"Yowwwl!" The pain, so much pain. My whole body feels like it is on fire from getting run over by that big noisy truck.

I bolt for the woods; at least I am still able to run. I hear the truck racing away up the street. Mom's just leaving the house when one of the kids runs up the steps. It's my next door neighbor, Mabel. She tells Mom, "Wilbur's been hit by a truck!"

"No!"

"Yes, he was."

Poor Mom, she's in such shock that she doesn't want to hear what Mabel is saying. Mom runs outside looking for me, but I am well hidden in the bushes and not coming out for anybody, not even Mom.

"Wilbur went under the tires of the truck that hit him, but then he got up and ran away," Mabel says. Mom sounds hysterical calling me, but I'm hunkered down in my hiding place.

She calls Rob to tell him what happened, and he says he'll come over to my house. Mom then calls her sister. Aunt Lyn has had numerous cats over the years and plenty of experience with these types of emergencies.

She tells Mom, "Wilbur will come home on his own when he's ready. He'll hide out until the hoopla in the neighborhood dies down."

Mom wails that I'll probably die out in the back woods somewhere if she can't find me. Pacing the floor and wringing her hands, she is so upset.

Well, I don't want to die. So about an hour later, I go to the back door to be let in, and Mom's there waiting for me. I immediately race to the dark and comforting cellar where I know I will be protected from any further bodily damage. Mom bends over running as she tries to catch me before I get to freedom. Even with me limping, she can't catch me in time to prevent me from hiding in the basement. Mom's so mad: she could kick herself for not shutting the cellar door.

My hole in the basement that I slip into when I want to get away is way in the back underneath the floorboards. Being a quick thinker, I drop in there before she nabs me. Mom calls the emergency vet in the area because my vet's office is closed after 5:00 PM on Fridays. They say to bring me in. She's happy that I'm still alive (well, so am I!), but now she has to wait for me to come up out of my hole. Rob shows up, and Mom calls her sister to give an update while they wait for me to reappear.

Finally I decide to come up out of the hole. I lie down on a roll of insulation in the farthest corner of the crawl space. I'm not moving for anyone, so Mom has to come to me. Down on her knees, she crawls into the dark cobweb-filled space with my travel home in hand. She pushes me into the carrier; I am in no mood to protest. Not seeing any blood, Mom worries about internal bleeding.

Rob drives us to the emergency room, and they take me right in. It's good Rob is there because he calms Mom down. I am shaking and very stressed-out. The vet informs Mom that they are going to hold me overnight to make sure the painkillers take effect and to determine what is wrong. She leaves me—I can't believe it.

"Mom, please stay with me!" I cry. I am so scared.

The strange people shave my back and then put a sticky thing on it that instantly makes the pain go away. Aaahh. I conk out immediately and don't wake up until the sun comes up the next morning.

In the morning, Mom comes back to get me and is told that I have a broken shoulder bone, but no internal damage. Oh, hallelujah! She is so relieved she nearly collapses on the floor. Now she can breathe again, not having realized she'd been holding her breath while awaiting the results.

Wilbur's Story

Once again, I'm told that I can't go outside. The vet even tells Mom she should cage me so that I don't do any further damage to my shoulder. Yeah, like that's going to happen. Mom ends up locking me in her bedroom, where I hide under the bed for days. It's nice and quiet under there, not unlike the basement, though without all the cobwebs.

Mom brings up my food, water, and even my litter box. A cat could get used to this treatment, but not at the cost of such horrible pain. It's painful just climbing in and out of my litter box. At least there's no stupid cone this time. Each day I feel better and better, and, after a few weeks, I start rushing the door any time Mom goes in or out of the room. I graduate from the bedroom to the main part of the house, and eventually I am allowed to go down in the cellar or up in the attic. When I want to go back outside, I bite Mom to get her attention. She decides I'm healed enough to go back outside.

To this day, if I hear a truck driving down the road, I run for the hills. I don't go anywhere near that road, but play in the backyard instead. I love to have my shoulder rubbed where Mom thinks I'll get something called arthritis when I get older. The bones healed fine. The doctor says I could have an operation done on my shoulder, to the tune of two thousand dollars, but we cats are wonderful creatures in that our bones mend on their own. Mom thinks I am very brave for surviving the whole ordeal. I never want to go through that again.

Lany Williams

Wilbur's Story

Lany Williams

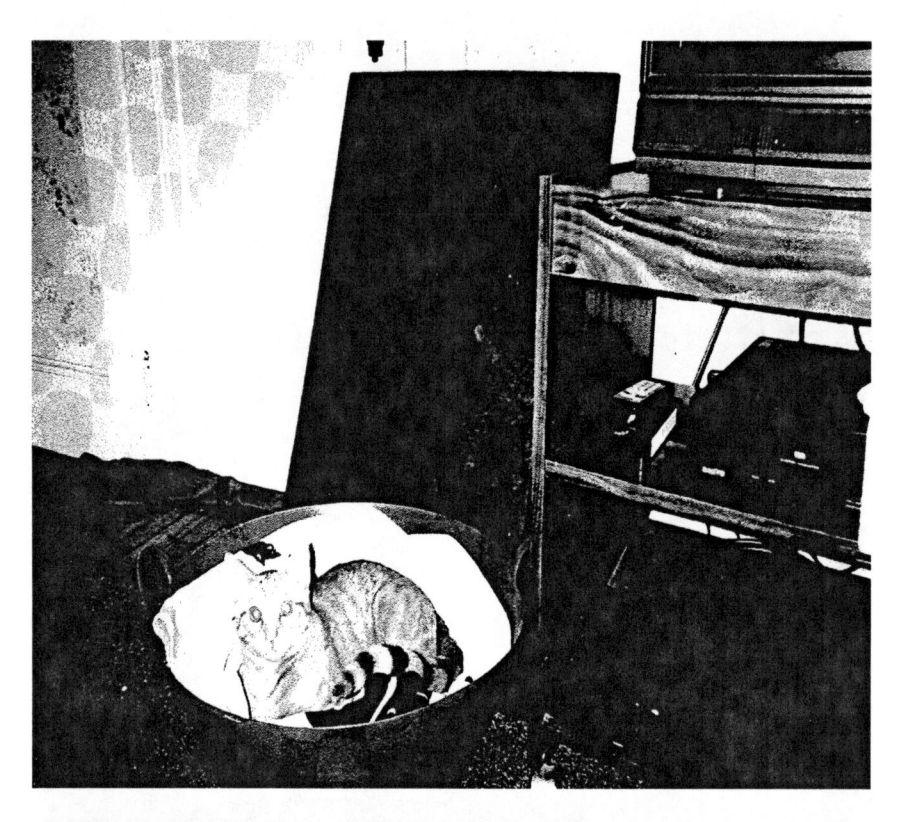

Wilbur's Story

Bird Emergency

In my younger days, I used to go across the street to Louise's as she had many bird feeders in her backyard. I'd sit under them for hours, just waiting and hoping to catch a bird (I was rather successful in that endeavor!) At our new home in Woburn there is no place to hang a feeder for my backyard entertainment. But there are lots of birds around: they live in the rain gutters on my neighbor's roof.

One day, Mom has old stale bread that she breaks up and *stupidly* tosses on the ground for the birds. Oh boy, a field day! When Mom goes to the back door to let me in, I come running with a bird dangling from my mouth—a present for Mom. She tells me to drop the bird and rushes outside to grab me. She's not happy with me, so I scamper off.

Mom discovers the bird a short while later on the driveway, dead from a heart attack. I don't eat the birds: they are nasty with all of those feathers. I only want to play with them, but the birds don't agree. Mom gives the poor bird a burial in the backyard by placing him under the azalea bush. The next day it's gone, so some other predator must have gotten him. Nature knows how to clean up after itself.

A few days later, Mom takes another bird away from me that isn't quite dead. She's heartbroken because she doesn't know how to save it. She throws me inside, grabs a shoebox to put the bird in, and sits outside with it until its eyes slowly dim and go out. She doesn't want it to be alone and afraid during those last minutes of its life. As I watch from the kitchen window, everything seems to slow down around her. Even the birds in the trees grow quiet while that poor bird gasps his last breath of air. Mom's so sad that she starts to cry. Watching the life go out of another living creature is very heartbreaking for her.

Not for me. I get the short end of the deal. Mom makes me wear a bell collar after that, so the birds will have a chance to get away before being pounced upon. I feel like such a sissy.

I'm having tons of luck catching birds. The bell collar doesn't last long. It's meant to snap off if it gets caught on something. By sheer luck, I find that I can get the collar to snap off by crawling through the bushes. So now I can make sure that collar is history soon after it's snapped on.

The last bird incident occurs shortly after the bird death in the backyard. This time the bird is still moving, but it is unable to fly away. Once again, Mom throws me in the house, grabs a shoebox (she has lots of shoes), scoops up the bird, and puts him on the patio table in the covered box so that no other predator can get it. This time, Mom calls my vet to see if they'll take in an injured bird. They suggest another vet who treats small wild animals.

So she puts the shoebox with the bird in it next to her in the front seat of the car and drives to the wild animal hospital. I don't get to go. Mom isn't worried that the bird will die, but that it will recuperate and try to fly away, possibly injuring itself in the box. I hear later that when she got to the vet's office, they took off the lid, and the bird just sat there staring back at them. The vet said she'd see what they could do, and Mom could call them the next day for the prognosis. She does.

Unfortunately, another bird bites the dust. It had internal injuries that could not be repaired, so the vet euthanized the bird. Mom feels so bad because she really tried to save this one. Because Mom is upset with me for catching birds, I decide not to catch anymore, just for her.

Cancer!

Animals are like humans; they can get life-threatening maladies that can break a mother's heart. Mom had such a scare with me. Every night and every morning we have our love fest of Mom scratching my back and chin. One morning, she's scratching my head and feels a lump on my cheek.

Mom's first thought is, "Oh no, it's cancer!"

Cancer can be a very scary thing. It could sound the death knell of a very young life such as mine. Again, I don't want to die. I am Mom's very special cat. Who will be there to purr and rub against her when she's happy or sad and lonely?

Mom immediately calls her sister, the cat expert, who says to call my vet and take me in to be checked out. Mom is so scared. So am I. The vet says to bring me in right away. Mom prays as she drives that it isn't cancer and that I will be all right. While Mom paces the waiting room, the technician takes me into surgery. I see all of the sympathetic looks from the other people who are waiting for their beloved pets to come out of surgery.

"Will I ever come back and see Mom?" I worry.

The vet shaves my whole left cheek and then removes the growth. Those three days waiting for the diagnosis are three very long, nerve-wracking days. The result is noncancerous. Can you say happy? The angels must have heard Mom's prayers. I give a big sigh of relief. The lump is a fatty deposit growth which happens often on animals. Why can't the vet

Lany Williams

world tell poor mothers that such things exist so they don't immediately jump to imagining worst-case scenarios? The growth may come back, so every morning Mom rubs me down looking for lumps and bumps while I happily purr away.

The Blizzard

    I love going outside in all kinds of weather. I don't care what it's doing outside; I just want out. For a couple of years we had some pretty bad nor'easters: those heavy-duty New England storms that make any living thing want to hibernate for days. Mom would go out with her blue plastic shovel that stayed on the back porch from November to April and start shoveling the driveway. I'd stick my head out the back door and look at her as if to say, "Come on, Mom, shovel the steps so I can get out and play."

    One year we had close to forty inches of snow. It snowed for days. The snow drifts just kept getting deeper and deeper. School was canceled, businesses were closed, and Mom was out with her trusty blue shovel. She shovels a path from the back door to the street, and I take off investigating this new white world. Lucky for Mom, Old Man Hill's son had come to snowblow his father's driveway. He volunteers to clear the end of ours where the plow dumped the snow from the street. The snowblower piles the snow up at the opposite end of our driveway near the back porch.

    I hear Mom shoveling our driveway from the neighbor's yard, so I decide to head back and check out the situation. I jump up on top of the fence between the two driveways, and, just as I am about to jump into the mound of snow left by the snowblower, I hear Mom yell, "Wilbur, no!" She could see that I'd land in that snowbank and never get out. But I decide to jump anyway.

Sure enough, I land in over my head. Mom rushes to save me, but it's difficult to run in forty inches of snow. It's like running in a pool of water: everything's in slow motion.

In the meantime, I yell for help, "Yowwwl!" I try to jump out of the hole in the snowbank, but I can't get a foothold. I'm sure I look just like a little jackrabbit jumping up and down, covered in snow.

When Mom reaches me, I look so panicked and wild-eyed that she has a hard time not laughing. I am so freaked that when she finally picks me up I huddle close to her. That whole ordeal is very scary. Not until we get to the cleared part of the driveway do I wriggle to get down. I race for the back door. After Mom lets me in, I spend the rest of the day peering out at her shoveling the front steps and sidewalk from the comfort and safety of the living room window. I am not stupid.

Angel Boy

Sometimes cat owners notice their cats staring intently up at the ceiling, even though it looks like nothing is there. Well, that is because we cats see things our human companions can't see. Ever since I came to live with Mom, I would see bright lights darting around the room quicker than I could ever move. I would usually freak out and bolt from the room, not wanting them to catch me.

Every night I sleep at the end of Mom's bed on a cozy fleece blanket. I get very annoyed with her if she moves her feet and upsets my position. In the middle of the night, Mom would sometimes wake up to find me sandwiched between her legs and making it very hard for her to move.

One night Mom is sound asleep when she feels a strong urge to wake up. The house is quiet as a tomb. She has the sensation of someone watching her, and the hair on the top of her head and arms stands straight up. At this point in time, Janie has moved out, and it's just the two of us, so there shouldn't be anyone looking at her in the dead of night.

Mom raises her head and sees a little boy surrounded by a bright white light standing beside the bed staring at her. She's shocked to see him. The boy is about five years old with short straight blond hair.

"What's your name?" Mom asks him.

She hears the reply, "Wilbur."

Lany Williams

Mom looks over at me, but I'm sound asleep on the fleece blanket, not having been woken up by our nighttime visitor. She looks back to the boy, but he's now gone.

Very spooky. Even a little creepy. I am so glad I didn't wake up.

Mom eventually falls back to sleep and doesn't have any further disturbances for the rest of the night. Mom now believes an angel child wanted me to come out and play. No thank you.

Wilbur and the Dangling Mouse

One December afternoon, Mom is in the guest room upstairs wrapping Christmas presents. I go in to check out what she's doing, but take off running when she tries to put a silly little Santa hat on me. I don't think so. Mom always leaves the attic door open for me so that I can go up and play; I dash up there to get out of her reach. Because the windows in the attic are low to the floor, I can look out over the world or lie on the floor in a patch of sunshine. It's my fort. I'm not up there long before I find a friend to play with.

"Oh look, it has a long skinny tail like the smaller ones have. Who knew they came in different sizes?" I muse.

From downstairs, Mom hears some god-awful screeching going on in the attic—and it isn't me making the noise. In all of the past altercations, I never heard a mouse make a noise louder than a tiny squeak. I guess this is no mouse.

Mom runs up the stairs and finds me staring down at something behind a bunch of boxes. I look up at her, then back down at the floor. She can't see anything from her position at the top of the stairs, so she scoops me up and carries me back downstairs, shutting the attic door for a good solid week.

When I do venture back up, I look all around, but find no evidence of my new friend. It may have been a baby squirrel, though none have ever been in the house before, and they have bushy tails. Mom fears it was a rat as her friend, Lauren, has just told her that she has rats in her basement. That's the last thing Mom wants me tangling with: they can be somewhat vicious if cornered.

A few weeks later, Mom calls me in from outside to come to bed. I snuggle with her for awhile, then I head downstairs to have a snack. Mom turns off the bedroom light around 10:00 PM and has yet to fall asleep when I jump back up on the bed. Usually I lie at the end of the bed on my soft blankie, but this time I am sitting beside her near the pillows. I'm not looking at Mom, but looking down at my feet instead. Mom rolls over and turns on the light to see what I am doing. She's so glad she is still awake as I have brought a mouse up to the bed—alive. At least it's one of the small ones.

"Wilbur!" Mom yells at me as she immediately jumps out of bed.

I look at her, and the mouse takes off. She screeches at me to get the mouse, but now I can't find it. Mom goes around the end of the bed to turn on the other bedside lamp. As she rounds the end of the bed, she sees the mouse hanging on for dear life over the edge. He knows I can't see him. Mom starts laughing so hard, even while shouting at me to come to the end of the bed. I'm still looking under the sheets and blankets near the pillow for my lost *toy*.

The mouse does a *drop and roll* onto the floor. Finally figuring out what's going on, I chase after it. The mouse dives behind the large cupboard opposite the foot of the bed. I get on one end, with Mom on the other. The mouse runs right at me. I snag it and run off, with Mom right on my tail. Yeehaw! This is fun.

While turning on all the lights in the house, Mom chases me down the stairs, yelling at the top of her lungs for me to drop the mouse. First she yells at me to grab the mouse, now she's screaming at me to drop it. I'm confused, so I drop it in the living room.

By now I'm pooped from all of the excitement, so I decide to flop down on the floor and watch as the mouse scurries behind the TV. Mom crouches down on one side of the TV to shoo the mouse toward me. When it scampers right at me, I just watch it dash into the closet. I'm too tired to bother.

Mom goes into the kitchen to grab the mousetraps she always keeps on hand, and there she finds the original site of carnage where the mouse fight began. Next to the toaster oven above my food bowls, things are strewn about on the counter. The stupid mouse had come out to investigate while I was having my late-night snack. Mom never heard all the fighting going on downstairs before it ended up in her bed.

Wilbur's Story

    She sets a trap by the toaster oven and one in the closet before going back to bed. Mom shuts me out of the bedroom so there won't be a repeat performance of the great mouse chase; she has to go to work the next morning. In the end, she catches two mice, one in each trap. Being the great mouser that I am, I am proud to say that Mom never hears or catches another mouse in the house after that night.

Baby Squirrel's First Outing

One warm spring day, I'm playing in the living room while Mom is watching TV when we hear a noise outside through the kitchen window and decide to go out and investigate. I think it is birds or squirrels talking to each other or, more likely, having a fight. I see a mama squirrel and a baby squirrel on the fence beside the driveway. I go outside to check it out. Mom doesn't think much of it, so she heads back into the living room to continue watching TV.

After a few more minutes of the same noise, Mom finally gets up again and looks out to see that the squirrels are still in the same place on the fence. Apparently what has happened is that the baby squirrel's leg has fallen through the slats of the fence and gotten stuck, so he is hanging upside down. His mama tries to haul him up and out, but she can't manage it. Mom decides to go out and see what she can do to help.

Well right then another baby squirrel climbs down the side of the house next door and sees me. Twins! This little one panics and falls off the side of the house, landing on the driveway. I am stunned, and I'm sure he is too. He gets up and slowly crawls away. The mama squirrel abandons the hanging baby for the crawling one to get him to safe shelter. Poor mama squirrel is so frazzled between her two babies. Mom and I go to inspect the fence to see what we can do to help the one that is stuck.

The baby squirrel chatters at me while trying to get a good look at me from his upside down position. His eyes are real big and look terrified; he even holds his bushy tail up to his face to try and hide from me. Mom goes back inside and calls the local wildlife vets. But it has just turned 5:00 PM, and no one is there. The answering service suggests she call the local animal control officer. Mom calls the local Woburn police to try and get the number for the animal control officer, but the police tell Mom he is off duty. The police say they'll send one of their officers to check it out. Mom can just hear the police scanners now, "Go to Campbell Street to check on a squirrel stuck in a fence."

When she comes back outside, we see the baby trying to gnaw the wood away from its leg to get out. I have visions of him gnawing on his own leg to get free. Ugh! Worried that Mom might harm her baby, mama squirrel hangs out a short distance away to keep an eye on all of us.

The police officer arrives about five minutes later. Mom had tried prying the slats apart, after putting on gloves in case the baby tried to bite her, but it was no use. The officer asks if she has a screwdriver. Mom runs into the house, down to the basement, grabs the screwdriver, and runs back up and outside. The officer then uses it to pry apart the slats. The baby hoists himself up on top of the fence and proceeds to try and scamper away. This must have been his first outing as he looks very wobbly on top of the wooden pickets. I'm just waiting for him to fall between the slats again. Once the baby seems out of danger, the kind officer leaves. Mom goes inside to keep vigil until mama squirrel comes back for her baby.

About ten minutes later, mama squirrel reappears. She and the baby make excited noises at each other. The baby wobbly follows the mother, makes it to the end of the pickets, and finally lands on the sturdier stockade fence. My entertainment was done for the day, so I decide to wander off. I wonder about the poor twin who had fallen from the house.

A couple of weeks later, I see the two babies bounding along the top of the fence, chasing each other without a care in the world.

Wilbur and the Coyote

On a sunny Saturday morning, Mom let me out as usual before breakfast.

"Ooohh, what's that?" I wonder as I peer under Mom's car. I get a tingly feeling as my fur begins to fluff out.

Right then, Mom opens the back door to let me in. My fur is fluffed from my nose to my toes. She has never seen every single one of my hairs standing on end—neither have I. I race inside, but don't run to my food bowl; I run from room to room and then stand at the back door to go back out.

Mom thinks, "There's another cat on his turf." But she hasn't heard any of the yowling there usually is during turf wars.

She lets me back out and watches as I crouch on the top of the back steps and look down under her car in the driveway. "Aha! The other cat is hiding under the car," she muses. I don't move or make a noise; I just fluff out all over again.

Mom goes out and bends down to look under the car. That animal is too big to be a cat. She hustles me back inside and then goes for a closer look.

"Don't get too close, Mom. It looks nasty," I worry.

Mom sees what looks to be a dog's leg, but then he turns his head to look at her.

"That's no dog. That's a coyote!" It has a long, thin pointy nose. He looks at Mom. She looks at him and says, "Okay," then heads back into the house.

I was looking at her as if asking, "What is that out there?"

"Wilbur, you're staying inside or else you're gonna be breakfast." Mom is horrified to think that I had been only inches away from that coyote.

Once again Mom calls the animal control officer. She thinks they are getting kind of used to her by now. The regular officer has the weekend off, but the substitute officer is on duty and says to hang on; he'll be there shortly.

Before he arrives, Mom walks around to the front of the house to get another look from a different angle. Yup, it's still a coyote. She thinks maybe it is hurt because it hasn't tried to run away. I stick my nose to the front window to watch all the drama unfold.

Once again a police cruiser pulls up in front of our house. Mom expects to hear "Crazy lady on Campbell Street has another animal stuck at her house!" As we wait for animal control, our neighbor, Mr. Hill, who's eighty years old, strolls down to see what all the commotion is about.

Mom tells him, "There's a coyote under my car. Maybe you should go home before it comes out and attacks you." Mr. Hill would never be able to get away, hobbling with his cane. By this time, Mrs. Hill arrives and a few other neighbors are strolling down the street. Don't they know that there is a wild animal just waiting to jump out and attack them?! Oh well, that's their problem.

Animal control finally shows up. The officer is all excited as he's never seen a coyote before. Well neither have I, until this morning. Mom asks the officer what he plans to do, and he says that he doesn't know.

"You're not going to shoot it, are you?" She gasps.

No. He goes and gets one of those choke-hold poles, then asks her to move her car out of the way. Now there are two strong men, a horde of neighbors, and Mom. Nobody's going near the coyote, but they're asking her to go over, get in the car, and possibly drive over an injured animal. So of course Mom says, "Okay."

As Mom starts the car, the officers check to see what the coyote is doing. Nothing. Mom pulls forward and makes sure the police officer can see if she's going to run over the poor animal or not. But once the car moves, so does the coyote. He runs for the hills, literally.

Unfortunately, my fenced-in backyard keeps him from freedom. So now the animal control officer says he's going in, but he needs Mom to open the gate on the other side of the house. The coyote tries to jump the six-foot fence, but stops to watch what Mom is doing as the officer sneaks around the other side to herd him out. Because the coyote looks healthy, the officer doesn't want to try capturing him; he just wants to get him headed back in the direction he came from.

Meanwhile, Mr. and Mrs. Hill, the nice police officer, and several neighbors are milling about the front of my house, chatting away. Mom backs away from the gate. The coyote shoots out from the backyard, then turns and heads right through the crowd of people.

Mom thinks, "This is it. Mr. Hill is going down as the weakest member of the pack." But no, the coyote keeps on booking it, right around the corner and past my other neighbor and her two-year-old son. They cry out, "Is that a fox?"

"No," everyone answers. "It's a coyote."

That coyote never looks back. The animal control officer says there is a pack of them living up the street in some woods at the end of a dead-end road. This one must have gotten separated from the pack while out hunting for food. With it getting light out and people moving about, the coyote was probably looking for a safe place to hide out for the day—right in our yard. I guess the animal control officer is right; you can live ten miles from a major urban city and still live amongst the wild.

Mom kept me in for many nights after that, but eventually I wore her down. She let me out again at night and almost thought she'd live to regret it the day I went missing.

Wilbur's Lost!

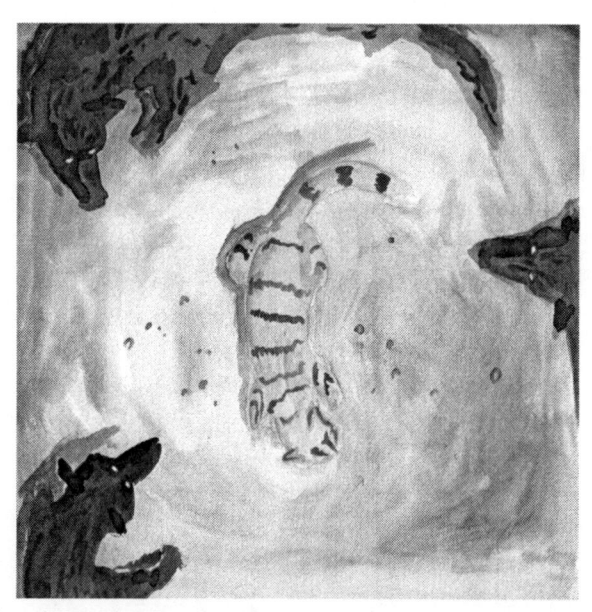

After the coyote incident, Mom is a bit nervous when I go out at night, but I always come in before she goes to bed. One night Mom calls me to come in, but I ignore her as I am not ready to go in yet. About an hour later she tries again, and I still don't come. Mom is worried, but the night is balmy, and I have stayed out all night in the past, so she turns out the lights and goes up to bed.

The next morning, Mom tries calling me in again, "Willlburrr!"

Usually I'm already at the back door ready to come in for breakfast, but not today. Mom goes through her whole morning routine and needs to leave for the office. At the very latest, I will come running when I hear the car start because it's my last chance to get inside for the day where my food bowl is located.

"Willlburrr!" Mom's beginning to panic. She even shakes the deli meat bag out the back door.

Mom decides to drive slowly around the neighborhood looking for orange stripes through the foliage. No Wilbur. She drives back home and calls the office to tell them she is sick and can't make it to work that day. She's so worried that she starts to cry. Mom doesn't know what to do as I've never been gone from home this long. She calls the animal control officer—he really knows Mom now!—and he tells her to call the local shelters and animal hospitals.

"Oh please don't be in the hospital," Mom prays, though finding me hurt is better than not finding me at all.

No luck. They suggest she walk the neighborhood checking garages and backyards. Mom decides to take another drive around the neighborhood and sees two ladies talking on their front porch steps. One of them says she saw an orange tabby sitting at the bus stop with the school kids that morning. He didn't go up to anyone, just sat a short distance away and watched the kids play. That sounds just like me.

Mom drives back home and gets in touch with the PAWS shelter in Wakefield. They suggest putting up fliers with my picture on it. Mom e-mails them one for their Web site (I now have a mug shot). Mom takes the fliers in hand and walks up to the Hill's house and asks them to keep an eye out for me. She even checks their backyard.

Then she crosses the street to look in my neighbor's garage, which is very musty with lots of nooks and crannies where a cat could get lost for days. She even tells Mabel from next door that I am missing. Everyone is very sad to hear the news. Boy it's great to be loved.

Mom cries off and on all day.

It is night, and I still have not come home. Mom calls her sister, the cat expert extraordinaire. Aunt Lyn suggests Mom put food out for me. When I come home, I'll be very hungry and will hang out by the food bowl. Mom thinks, "So would the coyotes," but she doesn't say anything.

Mom takes one last walk in the rain around the neighborhood with her trusty flashlight. She isn't too hopeful of finding me by then; it is just something to do. Mom starts reliving all my cute and exasperating moments from when I was a baby until now. Such fun, loving adventures we've had, and so many laughs I've given her. That starts her thinking about writing *Wilbur's Story*.

All Mom can picture that dark, rainy night is my body in the middle of a pack of coyotes being eaten for dinner. She visualizes my sweet face and loses hope of ever seeing me again or feeling my soft, furry body and my warm drool on her neck.

"Willlburrr!" She tries calling me in one more time that night before going to bed. Mom calls upon all her angels, and my angels too, to bring me home safe to her. She lies in bed promising to do anything just so long as I come home to her. She misses me terribly.

The next morning Mom gets up and goes to the back door, and who is sitting there waiting to be let in? Yes, me. I finally came home!

Mom is so relieved, like a weight has been lifted from her heart. I saunter in like nothing ever happened. I have no bite marks, no pieces of fur missing, no matted hair, nothing. I am ravenous, so I eat breakfast and then bound up the stairs to bed. Mom could've killed me; but she is so happy that I am home safe and sound. She scratches my ears, kisses me on my head, and lets me go to sleep.

"What's all the fuss about?" I think. I'd decided to stay outside a few extra nights because last weekend Mom left me locked up inside the house for two whole days. I was not about to be locked in again anytime soon. No sir.

Outside the food bowl is almost empty—great idea, Aunt Lyn! Mom immediately calls to tell her that I am home. Mom runs into the Hills, who ask if she's found her cat. Mabel is thrilled to hear that I have come home. The lady who saw me at the bus stop asks Mom if she ever found me. Mom is glad to tell everyone that my adventure had a happy ending. Even though I continue to go out at night, I always show up before bedtime—at least for now.

About the Author:

Lany volunteered one year at the Animal Rescue League shelter in Dedham, Massachusetts, and fell in love with all the animals. Right then she knew she needed a cat of her own. Lany lives in Woburn, Massachusetts, where she is an accountant by day and Wilbur's mom by night. An avid supporter of many of the local and national organizations that promote animal welfare, Lany hopes that many others will find their own Wilbur. Please visit her website at lanywilliams.com.